I0803371

STRENGTH IN NUMBERS: ANIMAL GROUPS

FISH GROUPS

BY HEATHER C. HUDAK

Cover image: Clownfish live in groups that include one dominant female, one dominant male, and several other males.

Core Library
An Imprint of Abdo Publishing
abdobooks.com

abdobooks.com

Published by Abdo Publishing, a division of ABDO, PO Box 398166, Minneapolis, Minnesota 55439.
Copyright © 2026 by Abdo Consulting Group, Inc. International copyrights reserved in all countries.
No part of this book may be reproduced in any form without written permission from the publisher.
Core Library™ is a trademark and logo of Abdo Publishing.
Printed in the United States of America, North Mankato, Minnesota.
052025
092025

THIS BOOK CONTAINS RECYCLED MATERIALS

Cover Photo: Kurit Afshen/Shutterstock Images
Interior Photos: Shutterstock Images, 4–5, 12–13, 19 (fish), 20–21, 23, 25, 28–29, 34 (fish), 36–37, 43, 45; Leonardo Gonzalez/Shutterstock Images, 7; Thomas Kline/Design Pics/Getty Images, 15; Jeff Foott/Photodisc/Getty Images, 17; Red Line Editorial, 19 (ladder), 34 (tanks); Reinhard Dirscherl/ullstein bild/Getty Images, 31; Wildlife GmbH/Alamy, 33; Gianni Cicalese/500Px Plus/Getty Images, 39; Joe Belanger/Shutterstock Images, 41

Editor: Laura Stickney
Series Designer: Ryan Gale

Library of Congress Control Number: 2024948986

Publisher's Cataloging-in-Publication Data

Names: Hudak, Heather C., author.
Title: Fish groups / by Heather C. Hudak
Description: Minneapolis, Minnesota: Abdo Publishing, 2026 | Series: Strength in numbers: animal groups | Includes online resources and index.
Identifiers: ISBN 9781098297268 (lib. bdg.) | ISBN 9798384919780 (ebook)
Subjects: LCSH: Fishes--Juvenile literature. | Fish communities--Juvenile literature. | Animal colonies--Juvenile literature. | Fishes--Behavior--Juvenile literature.
Classification: DDC 597.5--dc23

CONTENTS

CHAPTER ONE

HERRING

Hundreds of thousands of herring gather to form a massive school. It's spring, and the herring are on their way to their spawning grounds to reproduce. They begin their migration from the open ocean. The fish will travel to the coastal waters where they hatched. But they face many dangers along the way. Hungry predators, such as whales, dolphins, and seabirds, wait nearby to snatch up the herring.

There are about 200 different herring species. The most common are Atlantic herring, Pacific herring, and Araucanian herring.

HERRING FARTS

Scientists believe herring can hear the clicking sounds made by whales, dolphins, and porpoises. They can also hear other herring passing gas bubbles through their rear ends. These fart sounds are called Fast Repetitive Ticks (FRTs), and they are heard only at night. Scientists think herring use FRTs to call to each other in the dark. This way, they know which way to swim. During the day, herring communicate using visual cues. The more herring there are in a school, the more FRTs they make. Most predators cannot hear FRTs.

Most herring are between 8 and 15 inches (20 and 38 cm) long. They move through the water at up to ten times their body length per second. As the herring swim, their bodies move in unison. Every movement in the school is synchronized.

The school is densely packed. The herring stay close together to lower their chances of being eaten. If a herring swims off on its own, it likely won't live long. After the herring spawn, the school will spread out.

Herring balls are sometimes called bait balls. As a herring ball rotates, each fish tries to get closer to the ball's center.

Feeding will become the top priority, and fewer fish means less competition for food. But for now, there is safety within the massive group.

Suddenly, a humpback whale appears beneath the school. The herring swim quickly, trying to confuse and escape the predator. But the whale isn't alone. Several humpbacks encircle the school. They slap their tails on the surface of the water to scare the herring. Then they release bubbles that form a curtain around the school.

The frightened herring move closer together to form a rotating ball. They are packed so tightly that they look like a single organism. The bubble curtain acts like a net, containing the herring inside. Fish near the center of the ball are more protected than fish on the outside.

The herring ball swirls toward the water's surface. Overhead, gulls swarm the herring ball. They dive at the water, plucking out herring one by one. Below the surface, humpbacks lunge at the herring ball with open mouths. When they've had their fill, the whales swim away. The remaining herring continue their journey.

At the spawning grounds, each female lays 30,000 to 200,000 eggs. Then the males fertilize them. The more eggs there are, the better the chances that some of them will survive. The herring swim back out to sea. The eggs hatch a few weeks later. The baby herring spend the summer growing. Then they make the long journey into the open ocean to feed, just like their parents.

FORMING GROUPS

Like herring, many types of fish form schools. A school of fish is a social organization. Most fish in a school are about the same age and size. They swim at the same speed and in the same direction. Their bodies are parallel, and the space between each fish is the same. If one fish turns, so do all the others. This happens so quickly that it appears as if all the fish turn at the same time.

Schools of fish are self-organizing. This means the fish gather on their own. Fish at the front of the school lead the group. When they turn, fish on the school's sides are at the front. They take the lead.

Fish in a school communicate using sight and sound. Fish have an organ along the sides of their bodies. It is called the lateral line. This special

SILVER DARLINGS

Herring are sometimes called silver darlings. This is because they have silver scales on their sides and bellies. The scales reflect light underwater, much like mirrors do. When looking up at the fish from underwater, the scales sparkle like the bright surface above. The fish blend in. This confuses predators, which helps the school survive.

organ helps fish sense small changes in water pressure. For example, fish in the school might change speed or direction. The other fish feel this change and respond accordingly.

Schools are not the only kind of group that fish form. Some fish form shoals. A shoal is a cluster of fish that swim close together. A shoal of fish doesn't move in unison like a school of fish does. Each fish in the shoal can do whatever it wants. A shoal can also include different species, while all fish in a school are the same species.

Fish swim in schools or shoals for several reasons. Most do it for survival. Swimming in schools helps fish stay safe from predators. The more fish in a school, the more eyes there are to search for threats and food. It is also easier for fish to find mates in a school. This helps more fish reproduce. No matter why fish form groups, one thing is certain. There's strength in numbers.

STRAIGHT TO THE SOURCE

Kali Wexler is a nature photographer. Every year, he takes photos of the herring run near Hornby Island in British Columbia, Canada. He spoke about how herring are important to wildlife in the area:

> *Last year, we hung around the water for two weeks before the big spawn happened. There was so much wildlife! We had almost daily . . . orca activity, which was awesome. They were there for the pinnipeds, which were also hanging out and waiting—sea lions, Steller and California, but also lots of seals. There were seabirds and shorebirds. There are bears and tons of eagles. So you realize the importance of the herring run [—they're vital] to the food web.*

Source: Sarah Brown. "Documenting the Herring Run." *Canadian Geographic*, 23 Feb. 2024, canadiangeographic.ca. Accessed 1 Sept. 2024.

WHAT'S THE BIG IDEA?

Take a close look at this passage. What is the main connection being made between the herring run and animals' feeding behavior? What can you tell about the relationship between herring and their predators according to this excerpt?

CHAPTER TWO

SALMON

Most fish live in either salt water or fresh water. But salmon are anadromous. This means they can survive in both types of water. Salmon are born in freshwater streams and rivers. They may stay in these environments for months or years. Then they migrate to the ocean to grow into adults. After a few years there, salmon return to the streams and rivers where they were born in order to spawn.

Every year, migrating sockeye salmon jump over Brooks Falls in Alaska's Katmai National Park and Preserve to make it to their spawning grounds.

ANADROMOUS ADAPTATIONS

Most fish would die after moving from a freshwater to a saltwater habitat. But salmon have adapted to survive this change. When a young salmon swimming to the ocean first reaches the salty water at the edge of its freshwater habitat, it waits there for a few days. This gives the salmon's body time to adjust. The fish drinks fresh water to prevent dehydration from the salt water. Its kidneys start to produce less urine. Salmon also have a pump in their gills that changes direction. It pumps salt out of the salmon's blood and into the water. When adult salmon journey back to their home waters, they wait for a few days at the edge of the sea to let the changes to their bodies reverse.

A salmon's journey to its spawning grounds can be long. Some salmon species swim more than 2,000 miles (3,220 km). They face many challenges along the way. They must swim through waterfalls, escape predators, and overcome man-made obstacles such as dams and fences.

Some salmon species use their sense of smell to find their spawning grounds. At least one species imprints on Earth's

Female salmon lay eggs in gravel nests called redds. Salmon eggs come in a range of colors, including yellow, orange, and red.

magnetic field in the waters where it is born. This field surrounds Earth and is created by the rotation of the planet and its core. Later, the magnetic field acts as a compass to guide the salmon back home.

Salmon lay between 2,000 and 10,000 eggs, but fewer than 1 percent reach maturity due to predators. The more eggs that salmon lay, the better the chance some will survive. Some adult salmon die a few weeks or days after spawning. Others journey back to the ocean for another season.

BETTER TOGETHER

In the ocean, salmon form loose schools to help them stay safe. The larger the school, the less risk each salmon has of being caught by a predator. This is because the salmon work together to detect threats and confuse predators.

Scientists at the University of Washington studied salmon schools. They used huge nets to scoop up fish in an area. Then they looked at the number of fish in each group and the size of each fish. They also looked at wounds from predator attacks and how much food was in each fish's stomach. The scientists found that salmon in larger groups had fewer wounds. This meant that the more salmon there were in a school, the lower the chance of any one salmon being attacked. In one case, scientists noticed that an increase of 100 salmon in a school cut the risk of a predator attack by 50 percent. Salmon that were larger or smaller than others were more likely to be attacked. This is probably because salmon that stand out are easier for predators to track.

Salmon that were born in the same river often stay in schools together.

However, scientists also learned there might be a downside for salmon in schools. Some species had less food in their stomachs than fish in smaller groups. These species typically travel farther into the ocean than other species. Food is harder to find in the open ocean. The larger the group, the more competition there is for each meal. Salmon that don't get as much food don't grow as big as others, putting them at risk of being spotted by predators. Still, the fish seem willing to go without as much food because it's safer to stay in the group.

SOCIAL CUES

Sometimes salmon don't find their way back to the spawning grounds where they were born. Earth's magnetic field shifts over time, and humans change the landscape. This can make it hard for salmon to know which way to go. Sometimes they get lost along the way. Because salmon are social creatures, they often work together to make decisions.

Salmon take cues from others in their group. When one fish swims in a certain direction, others follow. For example, salmon detect the scent of their home waters to find their way back. But sometimes the odor is not strong enough.

SENSE OF SMELL

Salmon have a strong sense of smell. It's so strong that a salmon can detect just one drop of a specific odor in 6.6 million gallons (25 million L) of water. When they are born, salmon imprint on the chemicals and scents in their surroundings. They also learn the smell of the ocean near the waters where they were born. The fish follow their noses to find their way home to spawn.

FISH LADDERS

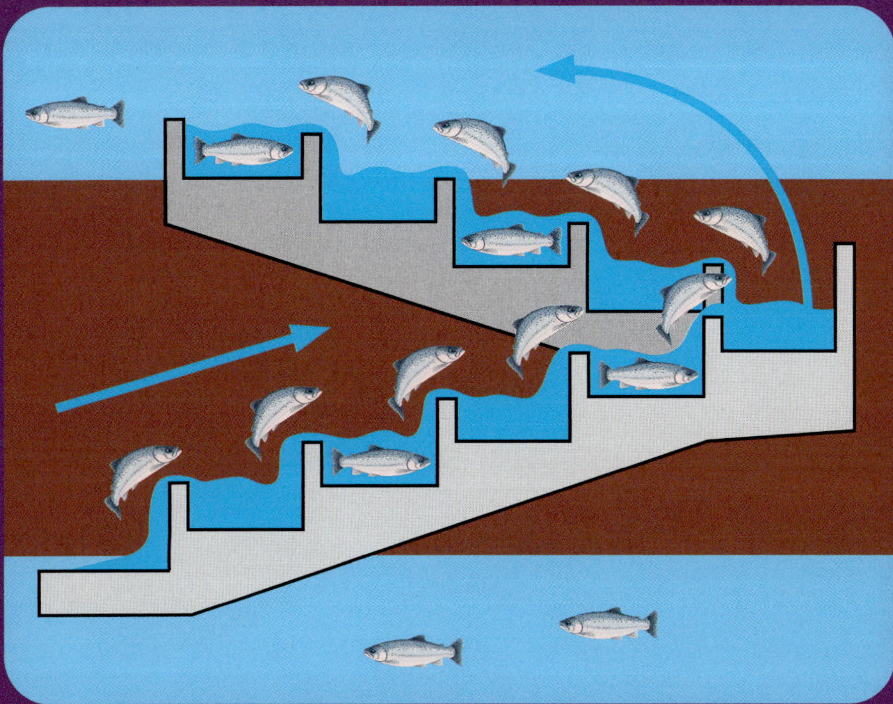

Some people build fish ladders to help fish travel. A fish ladder is a series of pools built like steps. It helps fish get around obstacles, such as waterfalls or dams. Fish leap from one pool to the next. How do you think fish ladders help fish survive?

The salmon must decide which route to take. They gather in the direction they think is correct. This acts as a vote. The direction with the most salmon wins. Salmon in smaller groups might not know enough to make a good decision. They are more likely to swim the wrong way.

CHAPTER THREE

PIRANHAS

Piranhas are freshwater fish that live in South America. They are commonly found in rivers and lakes in the Amazon River Basin. These sharp-toothed fish have a reputation for being dangerous predators. Horror movies and urban myths often depict piranhas as vicious pack hunters that take down humans and large animals. But there is little proof of this. The truth is that piranhas are shy, timid fish.

A piranha shoal may be larger or smaller depending on how many predators are in an area. In places where piranhas are more vulnerable, they form larger shoals.

Piranhas are omnivores that eat whatever they can find easily, such as plants and fruit. They also eat animals smaller than themselves, such as insects, worms, and small fish. Sometimes a piranha takes a bite off the fins or scales of another fish as it passes by, and the injured fish swims away freely to heal. Piranha attacks on humans are very rare.

BIG BITE

Piranha means "tooth fish" in the Tupi language, from what is now Brazil. Piranhas have small teeth. They are only about 0.16 inches (4 mm) long, but they are razor-sharp. When a piranha chomps down, its top and bottom teeth form an interlocking pattern. Piranhas have one of the strongest bites of any bony fish species. They can bite through bones and steel rods. A piranha's teeth are replaced throughout its lifetime.

PACKS OF PIRANHAS

Some piranha species, such as black piranhas, prefer to be alone. They might form shoals to defend themselves if they feel threatened. But they don't hunt in shoals. Most of the time, black piranhas stay out of

During the dry season, piranhas can get trapped in pools when water levels in rivers decrease. This makes it easier for predators such as caimans to catch them.

each other's way. Other species, such as the red-bellied piranha, travel in shoals of 20 fish or more. Some shoals include more than 100 piranhas.

Being in a shoal helps keep piranhas safe from predators. Common predators include river dolphins, caimans, and birds. Piranhas make barking noises when faced with a threat. These quick calls scare off predators and let them know the piranhas are ready to fight back. Piranhas may also make noises to warn their shoal mates about dangers.

Piranha shoals have a hierarchy. The leader is larger and more aggressive than the other piranhas. Older, larger piranhas swim in the center of the shoal, while younger, smaller piranhas swim at the edges where they are more likely to be attacked. The lead piranha gets the best spot in the shoal and gets to eat first. All the other piranhas obey the leader. If they do not, the leader might wound them or chase them off.

Piranhas sometimes attack each other. However, they still find safety in numbers. In 2005, scientists collected red-bellied piranhas and put them in an underwater cage in their natural habitat. They separated the piranhas into small groups. Then they faked a predator attack on each group. They measured how fast each piranha's operculum opened and closed to see how stressed it was during the attack. The operculum is a small flap that covers a fish's gills.

The scientists found that piranhas in the shoal were less stressed than solitary piranhas. The larger the shoal, the safer the fish felt. Scientists also discovered that

Piranhas usually have about ten triangular teeth per jaw. These teeth are covered by fleshy lips.

larger shoals of piranhas calm down more quickly after a predator attack.

FEEDING FRENZY

Red-bellied piranhas spread out from their shoal to look for their next meal. They use their strong sense of smell to find food and prey. They can sense a drop of blood in 53 gallons (200 L) of water.

Red-bellied piranhas also have excellent hearing. They are drawn to noise, such as the sound of a nut or fruit falling into the water. Sometimes red-bellied piranhas come across an animal that is already dead.

COW KILLERS

In 1913, former US president Theodore "Teddy" Roosevelt traveled to South America. There, he saw a shoal of piranhas eat an entire cow in just a few minutes. What he didn't know at the time was that this was not normal piranha behavior. The locals put on a show for Roosevelt. They had captured the piranhas earlier and kept them from eating so the fish would be starving. Then they threw a dead cow into the river with the hungry piranhas.

Other times, they hunt for food. If food is scarce, the piranhas might hunt a large animal that is old, weak, wounded, or sick. When this happens, the fish create a feeding frenzy.

During feeding frenzies, piranhas communicate with each other. When one piranha finds something to eat, it signals to the others. Each shoal member then takes turns eating in an orderly manner. After one piranha takes a bite, it moves out of the way so the next piranha can have its turn. The piranhas move positions quickly and constantly, which stirs up the water and makes it look like it's boiling.

STRAIGHT TO THE SOURCE

In his 1914 book *Through the Brazilian Wilderness*, President Theodore Roosevelt wrote about his encounter with piranhas:

> *They are the most ferocious fish in the world. Even the most formidable fish . . . usually attack things smaller than themselves. But the piranhas habitually attack things much larger than themselves. . . . The piranha is a short, deep-bodied fish, with a blunt face and a heavily undershot or projecting lower jaw which gapes widely. The razor-edged teeth are wedge-shaped like a shark's, and the jaw muscles possess great power. The rabid, furious snaps drive the teeth through flesh and bone. The head with its short muzzle, staring malignant eyes, and gaping, cruelly armed jaws, is the embodiment of evil ferocity; and the actions of the fish exactly match its looks.*

Source: "How a President Propagated a Piranha Myth." *Greater Cleveland Aquarium*, 16 Feb. 2018, canadiangeographic.ca. Accessed 18 Sept. 2024.

CHANGING MINDS

Imagine you are talking with a friend who has read Roosevelt's book and thinks piranhas are vicious, dangerous fish. How would you change your friend's mind? Make sure you explain your opinion. Include facts and details that support your reasons.

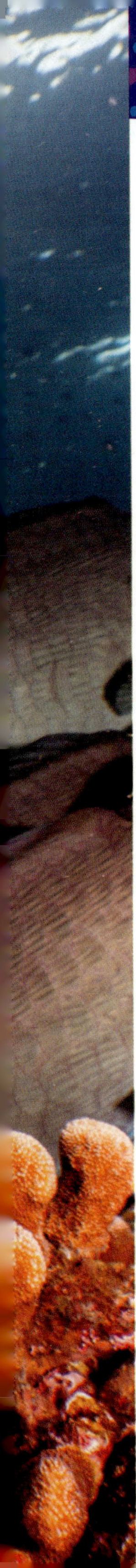

CHAPTER FOUR

SHOALING REEF FISH

Coral reefs are diverse ecosystems found in both warm, shallow coastal waters and the cold, dark depths of the ocean. They provide food, shelter, and safe hiding places for about a quarter of the fish in the ocean. Damselfish, parrotfish, goatfish, surgeonfish, and zebrafish are just a few fish species that depend on coral reefs.

Like many other fish species, reef fish often form shoals. Shoals may include one or several types of fish. One of the main reasons

One parrotfish species is called the bumphead parrotfish. These fish form shoals of 20 to 100 individuals.

for this behavior is protection. In 2022, scientists studied goatfish, surgeonfish, and parrotfish at the island of Moorea in French Polynesia and at Palmyra Atoll, a US territory in the Pacific Ocean. While there are many predators around Palmyra Atoll, there are few around Moorea.

The scientists noticed that while surgeonfish formed more shoals at Palmyra Atoll, they formed larger shoals at Moorea. This might be because surgeonfish in shoals work together to take over the territories of other fish, which helps them find food. Smaller shoal sizes at Palmyra Atoll might

FISH FOOD

Scientists studied the differences in the behaviors of shoaling surgeonfish compared to individual surgeonfish at several reef sites around Moorea and Palmyra Atoll. They found that surgeonfish in shoals traveled farther and covered more territory than individual surgeonfish in the same reef. The fish in shoals also had a fixed diet, while the individual fish changed their diet based on what food was available.

There are about 250 damselfish species worldwide. Many of them, including the sergeant major damselfish, *pictured*, form shoals in coral reefs.

help surgeonfish avoid predators, but this could come at the cost of finding less food. These findings suggest that predators likely play a role in the shoaling behavior of reef fish.

STRESS TEST

Some types of reef fish get stressed and lose weight when they are separated from their shoals. This might be because there are more eyes to look out for predators in shoals. When a fish is alone, it doesn't have the rest of the shoal to watch out for dangers. Scientists at James Cook University in Australia collected shoals of damselfish from the Great Barrier Reef. They placed an individual damselfish inside a chamber to separate it from its shoal mates. They measured the fish's metabolic rate, or energy levels. Then they put the fish in a tank with its shoal mates and remeasured its energy levels. The damselfish was calmer when surrounded by its shoal mates. It used about 26 percent less energy than when it was alone.

The scientists kept some damselfish separated from their shoals for two weeks. During this time, the fish used more energy because they

SAVING ENERGY

Scientists think fish in schools and shoals save energy by moving together as a group. For example, a fish can increase its speed by swimming in the wake of fish in front of it. Scientists at the University of Konstanz in Germany used fishlike robots to measure how much energy fish use when swimming in pairs compared to swimming alone. Fish in pairs used less energy because they timed their tailbeats to the wake of the fish in front. This helped them move forward using less energy.

Zebrafish shoals typically include both male and female fish. Some fish take on dominant roles in the shoal.

were stressed. They also lost weight. But when the damselfish were brought back to their shoal, they were soothed. Their energy levels dropped. When fish are less stressed, they conserve energy. They can use this energy for mating, reproducing, and growing. These all help the species thrive and survive for future generations.

LOOKS MATTER

One common feature of shoals is that different types of fish in the group often look alike. Some species select

CHOOSING SHOAL MATES

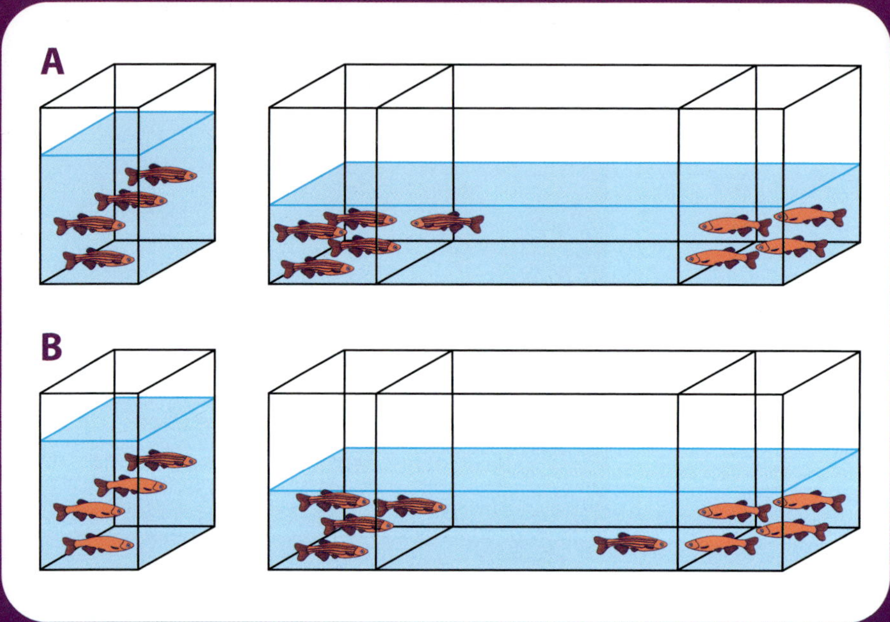

Scientists studied how zebrafish choose shoal mates. Group A was a group of fish that were the same color. Group B was a group of fish where one fish was a different color. A test fish from each group was placed in a tank. It chose between two groups. What does the graphic tell you about zebrafish behavior? Why do you think the fish behave this way?

shoal members based on factors such as family ties, body size, and species type. Scientists at the University of Texas at Austin found that a fish will choose shoal mates that look like the fish it was raised with.

The scientists put young zebrafish into groups based on their colors. In one group, a test fish was placed with other fish of the same color. In another group, a test fish was put with fish that were a different color. There was also a test fish kept by itself, with no other fish. Later, the scientists removed the fish from their groups so they could choose their shoal mates.

The fish raised in groups chose to shoal with fish that were the same color as the group they were raised with, whether it was the same color as them or not. The fish raised on their own didn't show any preference for one color or the other. This shows that early experiences and learned behaviors play a role when it comes to choosing shoal mates.

FURTHER EVIDENCE

Chapter Four discusses why reef fish form shoals. What was one of the main points of this chapter? What evidence is included to support this point? Read the article at the website below. Does the information on the website support the main point of the chapter? Does it present new evidence?

BACK TO SCHOOLING

abdocorelibrary.com/fish-groups

CHAPTER FIVE

BARRACUDA

Barracuda are fast, fearsome predators with big mouths, long jaws, and two rows of daggerlike teeth. They can open their mouths wide enough to scoop up just about any type of food they come across. This includes killifish, anchovies, octopuses, and small tuna.

Barracuda live in coastal areas in tropical and subtropical waters around the world. The great barracuda is one of the largest and most common species. It is a dominant predator.

A school of barracuda is also called a battery.

Great barracuda can grow up to 6 feet (1.8 m) long and weigh more than 100 pounds (45 kg). They have been known to attack humans, but these attacks are rare and often unintentional.

WORKING TOGETHER

Adult barracuda mostly live alone. Because of their size and speed, they have few predators. This means they don't need to be in a group to feel safe. But eggs and young barracuda can fall prey to sharks, tuna, and goliath groupers. Young barracuda form schools of hundreds or thousands to stay safe. The fish swirl in a clockwise direction to confuse predators.

SHINY OBJECTS

Barracuda are drawn to shiny objects, so they often hunt fish with gold or silver scales, such as herring. Light reflects off herring scales, making them appear shiny. Barracuda attacks on humans are often cases of mistaken identity. When humans have shiny objects in the water, such as jewelry or diving knives, barracuda might mistake them for bright, shiny fish.

Barracuda tornadoes have been seen near Green Island, Taiwan, and Sipadan Island, Malaysia. Chevron barracuda, *pictured*, are one species that often makes these formations.

This creates a tornado-like formation. It's hard for a predator to get its sights on any one barracuda in the tornado.

Adult barracuda sometimes gather together in cooperative packs too. They do so to improve their chances of catching prey. The barracuda scan the waters in search of their next meal, such as a school of smaller fish. They surround the school so the fish can't escape. Then they ambush it.

Barracuda use a technique called ram feeding. They slam into their prey at a high speed. Then they strike the prey and swiftly snap their jaws around it. The barracuda's top teeth stack on top of its bottom teeth, trapping the prey inside. The prey has no way to escape. The barracuda then shakes its head while using its razor-sharp teeth to slice the prey into pieces.

Barracuda have long, slender bodies shaped like torpedoes. This allows them to move through the water quickly. They can reach speeds of 35 miles per hour (56 kmh), making them some of the fastest fish in the ocean.

CLEANER WRASSE

The cleaner wrasse is a small fish that doesn't need to worry about becoming prey for barracuda. Barracuda have a special relationship with these fish. Barracuda float in the water with their gills flared and mouths open while the cleaner wrasse eat dead skin and parasites off them. This behavior benefits both fish. The cleaner wrasse gets a meal, while the barracuda stays healthy.

Barracuda have around 140 to 220 teeth. This includes an outer row of small teeth and an inner row of large teeth.

But barracuda can maintain that speed only for short bursts, so they save their energy for hunting.

Living in groups is an important part of many fish species' lives. Whether they form schools or shoals, fish work together to find food, avoid predators, and protect their young. This makes it possible for more fish to survive and thrive.

EXPLORE ONLINE

Chapter Five talks about the great barracuda. The website below goes into more depth on this topic. Does the article answer any of the questions you had about great barracuda?

GREAT BARRACUDA

abdocorelibrary.com/fish-groups

FAST FACTS

- A school of fish is a social organization in which most fish are the same age and size. They swim in unison, move at the same speed, and travel in the same direction.
- A shoal is a cluster of fish that swim close together. Fish in shoals do not move in unison like fish in schools do.
- Swimming in schools or shoals helps fish stay safe from predators. The more fish in a school, the more eyes there are to search for predators and food. It is also easier for fish in a school to find mates.
- During herring runs, hundreds of thousands of herring form massive schools. They form balls to protect themselves when threatened by predators.
- Salmon form schools when they migrate from the ocean to their spawning grounds. The more salmon in a school, the lower the chance any one salmon has of being attacked.
- Salmon work together to make decisions. They take cues from others in their group. When one salmon decides to swim in a certain direction, others follow.

- During feeding frenzies, piranhas communicate with each other. When one piranha finds food, it signals to the others. Each fish takes a bite of the food and then moves out of the way, giving the next fish a turn.
- Some reef fish get stressed and lose weight when separated from their shoals. This might be because when fish are alone, they don't have the rest of the shoal to watch out for predators.
- Adult barracuda form packs to hunt and improve their chances of catching prey. They scan the waters in search of food. If they find a school of smaller fish, they surround and ambush it.

STOP AND THINK

Dig Deeper

After reading this book, what questions do you still have about fish schools and shoals? With an adult's help, find a few reliable sources that can help you answer your questions. Write a paragraph about what you learned.

Say What?

Studying fish behavior can mean learning a lot of new vocabulary. Find five words in this book you've never heard before. Use a dictionary to find out what they mean. Then write the meanings in your own words and use each word in a new sentence.

Another View

This book talks about shoaling reef fish. As you know, every source is different. Ask a librarian or another adult to help you find another source about this topic. Write a short essay comparing and contrasting the new source's point of view with that of this book's author. What is the point of view of each author? How are they similar and why? How are they different and why?

You Are There

This book discusses piranhas in South America. Imagine you are traveling in South America. Write a letter home telling your friends what you see there. What do you notice about how piranhas feed? Be sure to add plenty of detail to your notes.

GLOSSARY

dehydration
when a body loses more water than it takes in

dominant
having power over others

ecosystem
a community of living and nonliving things in an area

fertilize
to join male and female cells to produce young

imprint
to memorize or mark permanently

migration
movement from one place or region to another

omnivore
an animal that eats both plants and other animals

spawn
to produce young in large numbers

species
a group of animals that can mate and have offspring

synchronized
happening at the same time

wake
the path or wave a fish leaves behind it while swimming through water

water pressure
a force that affects the strength of a water flow

ONLINE RESOURCES

To learn more about fish groups, visit our free resource websites below.

Core Library
CONNECTION
FREE! COMMON CORE MULTIMEDIA RESOURCES

Visit **abdocorelibrary.com** or scan this QR code for free Common Core resources for teachers and students, including vetted activities, multimedia, and booklinks, for deeper subject comprehension.

Booklinks
NONFICTION NETWORK
FREE! ONLINE NONFICTION RESOURCES

Visit **abdobooklinks.com** or scan this QR code for free additional online weblinks for further learning. These links are routinely monitored and updated to provide the most current information available.

LEARN MORE

Golkar, Golriz. *Freshwater Fish*. Abdo, 2024.

Parker, Steve. *Fish*. DK, 2022.

Stuckey, Rachel. *Shoals and Schools of Fish*. Crabtree, 2023.

INDEX

About the Author

Heather C. Hudak has written hundreds of books for schools and libraries. When she's not writing, Hudak enjoys traveling and has visited more than 60 countries. She's snorkeled with reef fish in the Caribbean, swum with sea turtles in Hawaii, and been on whale-watching adventures in the Azores, Mexico, and Norway.